Recipes for
HealThy Living

Copyright Julie Wandling 2003
Published by:
Hallelujah Acres Publishing
900 South Post Road
Shelby, NC 28150

The contents of this book are a reflection of the author's experience and are in no way intended to take the place of professional medical treatment. The author does not give medical advice or prescribe any technique as a form of treatment for physical, mental or emotional health challenges with or without the advice of a physician.

Acknowledgments

Thanks Mom for all your love, support and knowledge. Thanks Bob for helping me feed the kids vegetables. Thanks Boys for being my best buddies. Thanks Gramps John for happily eating my mistakes. Thanks Susie for giving the diet a try.

Thanks Judy, Paul and Kim for pouring over this work with me. Thanks Doug and Rozi for teaching me so much. Thanks Rev. Malkmus for the Hallelujah Diet. Thanks Dr. Fuhrman for the technical details. Thanks Miss JoAnne for pushing me to get tough. Thanks Dave and Val for being my "raw foods" pals. Thanks Chapel Pastors for the study of 1st Peter.

Thanks to my girlfriends who tell me when I'm looking good. Thanks to my tennis friends and coaches for playing with me. Thanks to the Health Seekers who come to our meetings and dinners. Thanks to my Yahoo Diet Club for supporting each other.

Thank you Lord for leading me to The Hallelujah Diet & Lifestyle.

FOREWORD

On April 21, 2001, I was conducting a seminar in the Park Hotel in Warren, Ohio. Over 300 people had gathered in a facility designed to seat 250 people to hear me lecture on the subject 'How to Eliminate Sickness.' Because of this overflow crowd, people were standing all around the perimeter of the auditorium, and even sitting on the floor across the platform where I was speaking. As I normally do, during the opening part of the seminar, I asked for testimonies from people who had been helped by the Hallelujah Diet.

Sitting along the center aisle of the auditorium, toward the back on the right side, a young lady stood to her feet to share what The Hallelujah Diet had done for her. She shared how she had lost almost 100 pounds, in a little over one year, since going on the Hallelujah Diet. After the seminar, I had the privilege of meeting this young lady and learned that her name was Julie Wandling. Julie was very bubbly and excited and shared with me her personal experiences on The Hallelujah Diet. I encouraged her to come to Health Minister Training.

Well, Julie did come to Health Minister Training and has been a strong advocate of the Hallelujah Diet ever since, and a beautiful example of what determination and a changed diet can do in a person's life. Julie, a Home School mom, has been very active in sharing The Hallelujah Diet with other Home School mothers, as well as with anyone else who will listen.

Not long after becoming a Health Minister, Julie wrote her first book titled: THANK GOD FOR RAW, in which she shared her testimony of physical improvements, along with numerous raw recipes. Many have been helped and blessed with the information and recipes contained in her book. Now, Julie has written a new book as a follow up to her first book, with many new recipes.

When Julie asked me to write this foreword, she asked if I would explain the Hallelujah Diet. That is a pretty tall order, because it is difficult to compress into a small amount of space all that is involved, but I will do my best.

THE HALLELUJAH DIET

The basic premise of The Hallelujah Diet is that the physical body we each possess is a LIVING organism, comprised of LIVING cells, and designed by God to be nourished with LIVING (RAW) food! When we look to nature, we find that every animal in the wild since creation to this present day, whether vegetarian or carnivorous, has eaten its food in its NATURAL, RAW, LIVING form! Only man, before he puts food into his mouth, puts that food on a fire, destroying all its life force (enzymes), and a high percentage of the nutritional value.

The Hallelujah Diet is a diet that is 85% raw fruits and vegetables. We do allow 15% of our food to be in the cooked form (baked potatoes, brown rice, steamed vegetables, whole grain pastas, baked sweet potatoes, baked squash, etc.), as we have found this small amount of cooked carbohydrates in the diet makes it easier for the average person to stick with the diet. We also use freshly extracted vegetable juices and a powdered Barley grass product. These raw vegetable juices are the quickest way I am aware of to rebuild our immune systems and essential organs, keeping them functioning at optimal levels.

With that said, let me encourage you now to sit back and read the beginning of Julie's book, as she shares her three-year experiences on The Hallelujah Diet! Then go on to incorporate some of her delicious recipes into your everyday meal planning. You will find many of these recipes to be not only delicious, but also nutritious!

Rev. George H. Malkmus, Lit.D.

Founder of Hallelujah Acres

Table Of Contents

Introduction

Welcome to the continuing saga of my life on The Hallelujah Diet. Almost four years ago now, I discovered The Hallelujah Diet by Rev. George Malkmus. At the time, I weighed in at a whopping 315 lbs and I was only 35 years old! My blood pressure had soared to 199/100 and the pain in my chest, back and knees was debilitating. My mom, Gloria Eden, actually found and adopted the diet first, telling me how wonderful it was and that I should do it, too. Being a typical daughter, I didn't listen - at first. It took a mild heart attack to get me on board. Once I started reading and learning I was hooked for life. It made so much sense to me how God created my body AND the more I learned about the food it was meant to run on, I couldn't believe I had ever eaten any other way. This diet simply calls for feeding the body with plant foods-fruits and veggies, 85% of them raw and up to 15% of them cooked. We like to call the 85% raw part the Hallelujah Part!

Creating new recipes has always been a hobby for me. Working in the foodservice industry for several years gave me an appreciation for taste and presentation of foods. A great challenge to my creativity came when I adopted The Hallelujah Diet. After two weeks of eating the same salad every night it was time to make this diet fun! Thank God for RAW, my first book, contains all the recipes I came up with the first year and a half on the diet-the ones that worked anyways! The majority of recipes in this book are for more yummy raw foods. I did add a section of "not all raw" recipes for those using the 15% portion of the diet that is cooked and for those transitioning to an all raw diet. All of the recipes are vegan.

I have now lost 120 lbs and maintained that loss for 2 years! The statistics are against me maintaining it but I know that with The Hallelujah Diet and God's Grace I will! I pray that my story and the recipes in this book will help you on your journey to health!

HOW BIG IS YOUR "WANNA?"

That's a line from a great book by my Pastor, Knute Larson, titled "The Great Human Race."

He reminds us that we all have choices to make, every day. Life is tough, no doubt, but we have unlimited potential. God gave it to us along with the ability to reason and make choices. Christ comes alongside us when we are tiring or getting down. So,

How bad do you wanna get healthy, feel good?

How bad do you wanna be slimmer, stronger?

How bad do you wanna play with your kids or grandkids?

How bad do you wanna do a handstand?

What are you willing to do to achieve it?

When Dr. Doug Graham was here last August, he was in Mom's backyard doing handstands. "I wanna do a handstand again," I whined.

He says, "So, show me your handstand." I thought to myself, "Yeah, right, what handstand? It's been 20 years since I even attempted a handstand! I'm afraid I'll fall on my face... literally."

He says, "Girl, if you wanna do a handstand you have to try. Try it 25 times a day until you get it, then practice it 25 times a day!"

Ok, here it goes. I get one leg off the ground, the other is glued to the grass! I'm cracking up laughing, along with my kids, and he says, "Great, try it again!"

More than 25 attempts later my arms and chest felt stronger... so much stronger! So, I keep trying until I get it! I'm getting closer each time to holding both legs up there and my arms are getting awesomely strong... I feel it!

So, how big is your wanna?

3

"Girl, it's a Flesh Issue!"

Mom and I went to Health Minister Training in July of 2000 with a friend, Roxanne. I whined I could have a whole houseful of fruits, but I wanted french fries so bad I wanted to walk for them at midnight. If someone would offer me a brownie, I'd want it so bad I could taste it. Roxanne would say, "Girl, it's a flesh issue."

It's amazing how many "flesh issues" I have. There have been so many times these past four years on the program that I just downright had to have something like mashed potatoes with salt… sour cream… cream cheese… butter! I knew they would not help me meet my goals but I also knew I would thoroughly enjoy eating them. At the time, my taste buds were so over stimulated that fresh foods had no flavor appeal. So, I had a choice to make… pleasure or health? The choice was mine and mine alone, and oh, what a battle!

Well, I am happy to tell you that after four years I still want pleasure, but its nature has changed. Now, for "pleasure," I seek out *mangos*! (I would love to try all 16 varieties!) It is so wonderful to experience pleasure from God's perspective. He does not deny us of pleasure – it just comes in a different package. And I know it's good because it is from Him!

When I first heard Rev. Malkmus speak three years ago, he was teaching from Romans 12. I had heard preaching on that chapter before but never from a health perspective. In the past it's been applied to problems around drugs and alcohol. I was shocked and totally convicted right then and there. His teaching on this chapter led me to our ministry name and the title of this book, Healthy for Him. I had tried to lose weight hundreds of times, hundreds of different ways but never for the right reason. When I discovered that the Lord wanted me to "present my body as a living sacrifice," I quickly realized that the best way to do that was by eating His food and exercising, following The Hallelujah Diet!

So, every time I want those stupid french fries, I remember my goal: to present my body as a living sacrifice to the Lord. It would not be a pretty presentation "overfat, greasy, weak, plugged up and rotting!" Therefore, even though I know I will never be the perfect sacrifice, I will keep trying to be the best sacrifice I can be.

"I beseech you therefore, brethren, by the mercies of God, that ye present your bodies a living sacrifice, holy, acceptable unto God, which is your reasonable service."
(Romans 12:1)

"What? Know ye not that your body is the temple of the Holy Ghost which is in you, which ye have of God, and ye are not your own? For ye are bought with a price: therefore, glorify God in your body, and in your spirit, which are God's." (I Cor. 6:19 & 20)

ONE STEP AT A TIME

This whole "get healthy" thing is a process. I have adopted this motto for myself:

"Every day, every meal, every bite!"

This reminds me that I have choices to make every day. I have to make a conscious effort to eat healthy... *every bite*! I used to take the fatalistic approach to my weight, saying to myself things like, "God just made me a big girl!" Or, "Love me the way I am!" Or, my favorite was, "If you don't like the way I look, don't look!" Now, when I hear women say that back to me, I want to cry because I know how they are hurting inside.

Yes, there have been many days in the last years when I have missed the mark, but I am learning not to beat myself up over it.

There was a time when I would make an unhealthy food choice and chuck the whole diet for months using that one handful of chips as an excuse. Not anymore. This time around I am getting it. No more guilt trips for me. I don't have time for it and it's certainly not worth the agony I was putting myself through. I knew that the more fruit and salads I ate, the less room I would have for other stuff. So, I kept eating the right things, over and over again. Stringing good days together is great because when you eat something unhealthy, you feel it!

The funniest thing happened - I now *adore* fresh fruits and salads. I can't imagine a day without a big green salad. Life would be so sad without pineapples and mangos.

I have become my own best cheerleader!

I tell myself, "I can do this... I love fruit... my belly is smaller... salads are my friends... I love to lift weights... I am a good person... I am disciplined... I am tough!"

There's a great book entitled, "Eating in Freedom" by the guys at FreedomYou.com. This is one of my favorites for learning how to root for yourself. They have taught me to change my thinking about myself... which is changing my outlook and my identity actually.

HEALTHY 4 HIM

When I climb a hill, I am a hiker!

When I play tennis, I am an athlete!

When I teach a history lesson, I am a teacher!

When I twirl my baton, I am a majorette!

And I'm good at it, too! Perfect? Not even close, but I can do these things and many more with practice, effort and determination!

It's so fun to play again!

Back to progression. I have been striving toward a goal – of being healthier and feeling good physically and spiritually. I wrote down my goals from the get-go. I learned that back in the 80's from my mom that I need to write them down, and I need to have "mini-goals" as well, to gauge (and make) progress along the way. For instance, one was to juice every other day. So, every other day, I make fresh juice.

Another goal was to be a vegan. So I *chose* not to eat foods that are from animals. After reading, "The China Project" by Professor T. Colin Campbell, and then meeting him at Hallelujah Acres and hearing his data firsthand, I knew this was a wise decision for me! (I have not failed on this one except for the occasional bite of cheese pizza – ugh - or feta cheese.)

Another goal was to exercise at least 30 minutes a day! A huge goal for this couch potato. That was so hard the first few months when I was feeling miserable at over 300 pounds, but as time went by and I kept at it, it became enjoyable *at times*. And while I have not loved the painful process, I love how I feel *after the hard exercise*! Anyway, the point of sharing this is that we have to try and then practice whatever it is we have set for goals. If small goals are more do-able, then set small goals. Strive to meet them and love yourself through the tough times. It's so worth the effort!

GETTING SERIOUS

I heard a pastor speak recently who said he often questions if a death was "the Lord's will or the lard's will." This sounds funny until you learn that even four-year-olds in this country have FAT in their arteries already. My dad ate Whoppers every day chased with Diet Coke. He died at 61 tying his shoes after a game of racquetball. *Was it the Lord's will or the lard's will?*

Sometimes I will see a person yet see through them. I see through their unhealthiness to the vibrant, healthy person they could be. Then comes the challenge as a Health Minister to help them see it, too!

I think the Hallelujah Diet is healthcare seen from a Christian world view. It's such a beautiful way to live and it's so simple and easy. I wish I could take everyone home with me and show them just how easy and wonderful it is. It is so cool to pick and eat apples in a field or sit in the sun amidst a field of strawberries *and eat more than you take home*. Or cut open a pineapple and enjoy its natural sweetness. Gifts for sure. And mangos... *I love mangos!* You know how you can eat at a restaurant and give compliments to the chef for that great steak? I get to do that with God every day, for every meal! Customers of my catering business used to tell me how wonderful a meal was and I would swell with pride (and fat). Now I can direct them heavenwards to compliment the Creator of the universe for all the wonderful foods He serves them. It's a beautiful thing.

Howard Lyman, cattle rancher turned vegan, tells us a story about supply and demand. We demand meat; the industry supplies it. We don't think about the consequences of our demands like rendering plants, nasty gunk from dead animals in our shampoos and cosmetics, crazy dog food, dying rainforests, etc., because they have to get rid of the leftover body parts somehow. It's not the industry's fault they have to ship cow dung out to sea to pollute our waters. We demand the meat, after all.

And water? We have a serious water crisis looming ahead. It's been in major magazines and on TV but we don't want to hear it. I am saddened to see what we as a culture are doing with God's gifts. I find people just don't want to talk about it, and they certainly don't want to deal with it, or consider a personal responsibility in the whole "circle of life." You can find his materials for sale from Hallelujah Acres as well as The

HEALTHY 4 HIM

Food Revolution by John Robbins. (I found them excellent, yet gut-wrenching.)

I know the environment will never be perfect again (and neither will we), but there is no reason to give up and accept mediocrity. Life is too precious, and fun!

ALL RAW?

For the last four years I have enjoyed long stretches of all raw weeks, even months at a time, but I have not been "all raw all the time."

I've gone through several phases with the diet myself so I understand that it is certainly a process. What I know for sure is the more raw foods I eat any given day., the better I feel.

Sometimes I am 95% raw and 5% Lebanese! I have a bent for vegan Lebanese food so I have it once in awhile. (Mmmm... hummus, falafel, tabouli...). This is still about where I am now but with many weeks and months of all raw thrown in for good measure. Living the Hallelujah Diet has given me so much freedom. No more guilt over food.

I know my boundaries. Fruits on one end and veggies on the other - with some nuts and seeds, even lentils, sprinkled in and around for good measure!

After observing a lot of people trying to eat healthfully, I think there are many acceptable variations within the realm of The Hallelujah Diet. For instance, those of us trying to lose weight may need to eat less cooked starches and fewer fats and grains for awhile. Folks with sugar issues may need to eat greens or celery with their fruit and add more greens to their sweet juices while lowering their fat intake. People trying to gain or maintain weight may do okay with the cooked starches or cooked beans in the evening. Still others seem to thrive on all raw with mostly fruits. We are all coming from a different place and heading in the same direction... toward better health!

I also know its interesting if not downright difficult to prepare a million different meals everyday! If your family simply will not give up some foods, find the best there is available and see if they will just eat less of it while increasing their consumption of fresh fruits and veggies. Then continue your education so you have the best information, and by all means, set the example.

The books, "The China Project" by Professor T. Colin Campbell and "Eat to Live" by Dr. Joel Fuhrman, are excellent resources for those of a scientific mind. My 12-year-old read both for science projects over the summer. I love to see the lightbulbs go off over his head as he reads!

Healthy 4 Him

I must tell you this great analogy I came up with while driving the car having a conversation with my kids. Ryan, 9, asked me why pop is so bad for kids. I'm always telling them not to drink the pop or colored drinks at church and parties, giving several reasons as to why not. Too much sugar, phosphoric acid, caffeine, rot gut, etc. We go through this conversation at least once a week. It has to be confusing for a young mind when he sees everyone else drinking pop. Even our local gyms and churches provide stuff that actually poisons us... amazing!!! Coca-cola was a dangerous substance for me. I know what it does to people. I see my friends crave it. I used to get such awful cravings for it, too. I would walk through the snow to the gas station for a two-liter bottle at 10:00 p.m.

Well, onto the analogy. I told my kids what Rev. Malkmus says, "One can of soda will hinder your immune system for three days." I told them, "You each have your very own super hero army in your bodies that is always on the job, fighting off the bad guys. But when you drink pop, you tie their hands behind their backs leaving only their legs to fight with for three whole days. So, for three whole days and nights, the bad guys have the advantage." They looked at each other and said, "oh that's *not* good."

OH YEAH! EXERCISE

Guess what? I still have to exercise! I play harder now than ever before! Not a day goes by without at least a 60-minute workout of some sort. I graduated to using exercise videos sometime last year and have had a blast with them! I have tried everything from Pilates to African Dance right in my own living room! I even tried belly dancing with Dolphina's Goddess Workout video! (I suggest, however, that you do it in private until you're good enough to show your husband, and keep the kids clear of the tv and you! It's not for kid's eyes. I forgot to mention that part to Grandma when she was babysitting one day. My boys were peaking at her and cracking up laughing!)

I started by borrowing tapes from the library to find out what I liked and then started purchasing them. One of my all time favorites is TAE-BO. Talk about having to push yourself. I call the TAE-BO Total Basic One tape the TAE-BO Butt Tape! My butt ached for days after doing that silly tape! I am up to doing some of the advanced tapes now but it has taken me an entire year of doing the basic tapes at least twice a week while doing other tapes and lifting hand weights the other days of the week. (Watch out for the rapid head movements Billy has you do in the TAE-BO warmups. When I first started doing his tapes, this really hurt my neck so I did them at half speed.) There is NO reason you cannot adapt any of these workouts for YOU.

Try contracting your thigh muscles without squeezing your knees. That took me 2 weeks to figure out! I learned from my "Power Yoga" book to hold those muscles and suck in my belly button while exercising and it makes me sweat buckets even when just stretching. The "New York City Ballet Workout" video and book are so great for working on balance and gracefulness that you will feel like a ballerina.

"Aerobics with Soul" is a totally fun series of videos I discovered at the library. I love the pilates tapes by Jennifer Kries and "The Method" and "Windsor Pilates" by Mari Windsor. My tummy feels so tight after doing her tapes.

I still love to swim but at the urging of Rev. Malkmus and Dr. Graham to "get out of that chlorine pool!" I switched to swimming in lakes, wonderful in the summer.

One thing I have learned is that when I take off a day or more, I get really stiff. The backs of my legs tighten up and then my back hurts. I feel less prone to injury when I am loosened up. To stay loose, I stretch every night. (My back hurt so bad four

years ago I literally lived on Flexeril muscle relaxers; I had a standing order with my doctor.)

I continue to set new goals. The goal for this year is to do back handsprings!

I got my handstand and cartwheel down now! (Thanks to Miss JoAnne at ALIVE Now Gymnastics, that is.) The beginning of 2003, my boys were taking gymnastics lessons. During their lesson a beautiful lady came in to coach a high school cheerleader. Watching them, I knew I needed to have her help me! I was so excited I ran down to meet her and ask if she would teach me gymnastics. She was so great. She didn't flinch at my weight or the fact that I was still very much out of shape compared to her cheerleaders (and her). I started lessons the very next week. The first thing she had me do was stretch which was right up my alley. She was happy with my flexibility.

She then handed me a jump rope and said "Ok, give me 100 jumps for your cardio. Try to do it in 10 minutes." She checked her timer and said, "Go for it!"

I learned in that very moment, that I could NOT jump. I couldn't even do it one time, getting both feet off the ground together. I just stood there staring at her.

She says cheerfully, "Okay, Beautiful! Let's try jumping on the floor trampoline now."

I got on the floor tramp, jumped four times and peed my pants! Mortified, I ran to the bathroom and came back to try again. This time I jumped a full two minutes. I was breathing from my toes!

Then she sits me on this big huge rubber ball (found out later its called a Stability Ball), puts my knees up against the wall and commands, "Now do crunches!" By the time she finished with me, I had done 180 crunches on that ball! I could not stand up straight for three days after that!

If it weren't for her enthusiasm and confidence in me, I would never have gone back. Miss JoAnne just kept rooting for me and pushing me to do the things I never

dreamed I could do. The next week brought more confidence, *and lunges*! Those absolutely awful lunges. When I would get down and didn't think I could stand up again, she'd call me "Grandma"! Another time she had me on all fours with ankle weights strapped on doing those nasty donkey kicks in five different directions.

A few months later, I finally tried the jump rope again. I started on the trampoline (and jumped for 20 minutes straight)! Oh, what fun! We just laughed. Then I moved over to the spring floor. It was much harder, but I actually jumped seven times! Now, I'm feeling tough. Every week, I tried a few more jumps until I couldn't jump one more time. Then I'd jog in place until I could jump again. My record to date is 1550 jumps in 30 minutes with jogging a minute every 100 jumps! Truly amazing. Sweat just pours off.

Eventually, I started doing the actual cheerleader warm-up. It only took me four months to work up to doing their *warmup*. Once I got that down she let me try a back handspring over the roly poly into a big squishy mat. Oh my... that was the most fun thing I have done! I did it another 10 times until I couldn't possibly do another, laughing the entire time. I finished each one just like a beautiful gymnast too - arms held high.

For those of you wondering, I am 5'10" weighing 190 pounds, down from 315 pounds. I am 38 years old with two kids. Now my goals have changed from losing numbers on the scale to dropping my body fat level.

I started taking tennis lessons too once a week with a couple girlfriends, Roseann and Sue, last winter with a local non-profit organization "Say Yes to Tennis - No to Drugs." Coach Solomon was so great. At first, he would hit the ball right to me so I didn't have to run when my knees hurt but I could still learn. This summer Coach Dan let me join in on lessons with the kids four days a week! He made me run once I proved that I could! I also played in a women's league one night a week and had a private lesson with Coach Robert another night each week - all summer long! I have a new respect for athletes and fitness-minded people. My kids have so benefited from this program that I want to encourage all parents to get their kids (and themselves) into some kind of fitness activity. We absolutely love playing tennis! My goal with tennis is to one day whoop my husband. He says it will never happen.

With my mom's permission, I share this with you. She walks like a drunk. She

always has. I remember walking around our hotel at Hallelujah Acres one night with her and she kept walking into me, in front of me, behind me. She couldn't walk a straight line for anything. She has always been this way. Well, in talking to many other women, I found their biggest fear is of falling. This led me to a study of balance.

What I learned is that balance can be improved at any age! You just gotta practice! So, I learned several exercises that are meant to improve balance. I am happy to report that mom is making great progress!

There are two kinds of balance: *static balance* is slow and deliberate; *dynamic balance* is moving balance.

You can practice it during your aerobic workout or any time you are moving quickly. Just freeze and hold it for a minute or so. I'm sure your kids or grandkids would love a game of "freeze tag!" It is amazing how you can feel every muscle working to hold you in place! Practicing static balance makes me feel tall and poised. You must hold in your core, bellybutton area, to hold a position therefore elongating the torso. I found some exercises in yoga books and ballet videos. (When we meet, ask me to show you some.)

Then I discovered quite by accident that when I squeeze in everything I can find, I am in more control of my body. I didn't used to be able to squeeze in anything! When I first started trying to exercise, I'd be squeezing and my squishy stuff would just be hanging there. That lead me to try isolating different muscles and holding them. Then holding them while doing another exercise entirely. I am truly fascinated by this. You know I had an incredibly hard, painful time walking up my steps three years ago. I cry when I see women in that place. It doesn't have to be so!

If you feel dizzy while practicing balancing or stretching, hang in there by holding onto something but continue in the pose. Slowly try taking your hand off and balancing on your own. When you can't hold it, touch back with your hand until you can. Just keep trying... over and over and over. And keep eating those beautiful raw foods. It is so worth the effort.

Sometimes when at my computer, I stand on one foot or with one leg outstretched until I can't stand the pain anymore. And then I hold up the other until it burns. If I have time, I go back to the other leg.

I have learned so much from Dr. Graham's cd, "Optimizing Your Training." He says I have to mix it up to get the results I am looking for. If I do the same thing over and over, like walking, my body will adjust and get used to the walking. What he has me do on my nightly walks is walk faster, walk backwards, skip, leap, do cartwheels, jump over my neighbor's flower beds (shhh, I missed a few times), all on the same walk! Certainly, my neighbor's think I'm nuts!

I can almost walk a whole mile backwards now without falling! I got a hitch in my get-along awhile back and decided to try jogging a little during my walks. I am up to jogging a full mile now! All I did was jog/walk/jog, making the jogging parts longer as time went by. I hope to be able to go five miles by Labor Day 2004 to participate in a run sponsored by our church. For years, Mom and I have helped serve fruit to the runners after the race. I like the thought of being among those who cross the finish line and stand on the other side of the fruit table!

Mom got me a real Needak Rebounder for Christmas! Hallelujah! Yes, I had to wear a pad at first while rebounding. (Sorry to say that guys. I debated whether to or not and thought it best.) It actually gets way better fast. Roz, Prof. Gruben of Healthful Living International and Dr. Graham's partner, said the motion will strengthen the bladder so leaking will stop entirely and also better prepare me for old age! Sounds good to me! No Depends necessary – *ever* - is my goal here!

Roz also taught mom and me "osteoblast exercises" for our bones. She had us clap our hands, stomp our feet, lift our rears and drop down onto a chair. She taught me chair dances, too. Great for folks who can't stand for long periods or much at all-everyone's gotta sweat!

I also want to highly recommend the regular use of a Stability Ball, those huge rubber balls. They offer comfort, while helping to improve overall balance and strength. Just sitting on it with your feet together is quite a core challenge. Miss JoAnne taught me hundreds of exercises to do with the ball. Then she got mean and added ankle weights! Most come with a nice booklet of excersises.

Once again Dr. Doug was right. "The best exercise routine is no routine at all." I have so much fun now with my gymnastics lessons, riding my bike with the kids, doing cartwheels after Sunday School with my kindergarten class, hiking, jump roping on my rebounder, and playing tennis!

EXERCISE SUGGESTIONS

I have tried countless video tapes from the library and these are my favorites—for novices to pros in that order, except where the levels are listed. Start with the basic and work your way to advanced. As I hit upon a favorite, I started collecting the tapes to have at home and use any time!

"Walk Away the Pounds" by Leslie Sansone - 1, 2, or 3 mile video tapes

All of the Richard Simmons video tapes

"TAE-BO" video series

"Aerobics with Soul" video series

"The New York City Ballet Workout" book and video

"The Method," "Perfect Mix" and "Three Dimensional Toning" by Jennifer Kries

"Windsor Pilates" by Mari Windsor

"Power Yoga" by Beryl Birch

"Zumba" with Beto

When you make your way through the Advanced versions, strap on some ankle weights and start over! You can then keep increasing the weight for a more demanding workout.

It feels so good to be able to play again!

HEALTHY 4 HIM

SUGGESTED EXERCISE STUFF

Ankle Weights - weight adjustable

Fit 10

Free Weights - several different weights

Jump Rope - swivel handles

Medicine Ball

Needak Rebounder

Quality Athletic Shoes

Stability Ball

Therabands

Water Bottle

Bath Tub & Candles!

TIME SAVERS

1. Eat whole fruits. It's very easy to tell the kids, "Grab some bananas and apples - it's time to go!"

2. Keep a healthy snack bowl. Ours consists of raisins, banana chips, almonds, cashews, sunflower seeds, pumpkin seeds, walnuts, pecans, apricots and whatever else is on hand. The kids keep it filled and emptied! I buy these foods in 5-pound bags, and then store them in big ol' glass jars.

3. Take good stuff with you. We have a food bag and water bottles that go with us everywhere we go. And I do mean *everywhere*. I have had people ask me, "Is that water bottle growing out of your hip?" I accept the compliment... two years ago I didn't even have a hip to carry it on. I will keep carrying my water and DRINK-ING it all day long no matter what anyone says!

4. Do the "juice thing." Juice three to four times a week and freeze it in eight-ounce canning jars leaving ¼" headspace for expansion in the freezer. Use frozen juices as ice packs for lunchboxes, and then drink it after it thaws.

5. Teach the kids how to do what you do... clean veggies, make juice, build the recipes. They will love the fact they're involved, and it becomes a way of life for them, too.

6. Make salad dressings a few times a week to have on hand. Store them in canning jars. It's so much easier to eat right when you have what you need when you need it.

7. Keep salads (mostly made up) for those times when you come home ravenous. Add a few items and you're ready to go. And it's fresh and wonderful!

8. Fill that nine-tray "Excalibur" once a week with munchies! Keep a snack size zip-lock full of your favorite nuts in your purse.

9. Buy the pre-washed baby greens in the one-pound bag instead of heads of lettuces.

10. Keep patés and hummus made in the fridge for quick and easy romaine lettuce sandwiches.

KITCHEN STUFF

Big Ol' Jars

Big Salad Bowl

Blender

Citrus Juicer or Reamer

Coffee Grinder - for flax seeds & herbs

Cutting Board

Dehydrator

Food Processor

Good Quality Knives

Juicer

Spiral Slicer

Water Purifier

HALLELUJAH DIETING ON A SHOESTRING...

Your juicer does not have to be brand new to get started. This summer we shopped thrift stores, yard sales, estate sales and the paper. We bought several juicers – cheap – and then gave them away or resold them. In the meantime, eat fruit in the morning when you would otherwise drink juice. If you want something new, save up for the "Juiceman Jr."... it is around $50.00 and does a fine job until you have enough for the "Champion." However, I must say that if you are dealing with a serious illness, juicer studies show better results from using the "Champion" or "GreenLife" juicers.

Dehydrator an issue? Use your oven. Just turn it down low and leave the door ajar. Turn it off, then on when it cools. Or, use an old electric skillet or wok set at 100 degrees. I used an old Ronco for the first year. The temp probably was not perfect but it was close enough for me. Again check out thrift stores, sales, papers etc. A friend got one for $5.00 at the Goodwill!

Looking for bargains on books and videos? Use the Internet in your search, and your local library. There are lots of raw food websites. You could read this one for days, www.hacres.com. I must say, the books and videos have been a wise investment for me. I read and watch and then do it again, all the while looking for new, creative ways to be healthy. "My people perish from lack of knowledge." (Hosea 4:6)

FiberCleanse – Hallelujah Acres is only recommending using this the first three to six months now anyways. Then move on to ground flax seeds daily. I have used the flax seeds all along adding FC only when necessary (usually when travelling). Flax seeds are only $1.00 per pound and the coffee grinder was only $5.00 from Big Lots. I imagine it will last forever using it just for flax seeds. (If you'd like another suggestion for constipation, try the rebounder. It's the best solution I know. There is no way you could remain constipated while rebounding every day!)

Organic Food - This is one area I didn't want to compromise often so I started a food co-op. If you are in the northeast try Northeast Cooperatives. In the midwest use Blooming Prairie or Something Better. We buy wholesale this way including produce, bulk nuts and seeds and lots of vegan junk food! Our 50-pound bags of organic car-

rots will be $24.00 this month! It only takes us two hours to do the work once a month for 35 families. When the produce from our delivery is gone, I shop the health food stores. Of course there is always gardening, indoors and out. I have sprouts growing now in the sink. Outside I grow herbs galore for teas and seasonings. Then I plant the garden all around my house in the spring. I had numerous entire meals from my backyard last year, and boy were they tasty!

Water - The cheapest way without an initial investment is to buy from a company that sells 5 gallon bottles like Clearwater or Distillata. We used to go twice a month and pick up 25 gallons. Now we have a Living Water Purifier from EcoQuest which is saving us a lot of money and providing us with purified water right at the sink.

Udo's Oil - Avocados, ground flax seeds, cashews, brazil nuts, almonds, filberts, macadamia nuts, pecans, sunflower seeds, pumpkin seeds, sesame seeds. These eaten regularly will provide great oils and fats (that are good for us, that we actually need). These can be used in endless ways! Check out some raw recipe books for dressings, snacks, cheeses, sauces, using nuts and seeds. I prefer to get my fats from foods. However, many people are severely deficient in the "good fats" initially and do benefit from adding oil in the beginning.

THe ReCiPeS

Spinach Lasagna
5 c cashews-soaked 2 hours
1 lb baby spinach
juice of 2 lemons
2 c sundried tomatoes
2 T mix of basil and oregano
½ tsp fennel seeds

NOT ALL RAW RECIPES

Spinach Lasagna
5 c cashews-soaked 2 hours
1lb baby spinach
juice of 2 lemons
2 c sundried tomatoes
2 T mix of basil and oregano
½ tsp fennel seeds

MEALS

HEALTHY 4 HIM

Nuggets

BOCA Nuggets or Quorn Nuggets
Bake according to package directions.
Great on salads with french dressing and the kids love them.

Note: Because these are processed foods, I only let the boys have them or something similar once a week or less. They are great for kids' parties.

French Fries

Cascadian Farms organic fries
Organic ketchup
Bake according to pkg instructions.

Ryan's Romaine Salad

By Ryan Wandling, age 8

Romaine lettuce cut very small
Black olives-sliced
Drew's Garlic Italian Dressing

Salad by Dad
romaine lettuce
carrot-shredded
tomatoes-chopped
celery-chopped
Frontier Bac'Uns
organic ranch dressing

French Onion Dip
Fantastic Foods French Onion Dip Mix
Tofutti Sour Cream or one jar raw cashew butter

Mix

Mexican Party Dip
1 can organic fat-free refried beans
2 tomatoes-chopped
1 container Tofutti Sour Cream or another avocado
1 avocado
1 can black olives-drained and rinsed-sliced or raw olives chopped
6 green onions-chopped

Add your favorite veggie cheddar cheese (or none at all)
Complete with your favorite organic tortilla chips or lettuce leaves.
Using a large platter, spread refried beans on first layer. Top with chopped tomatoes.
Blend sour cream and avocado in blender until creamy. Spread over tomatoes. Top
with olives, green onions and veggie cheese. Scoop with chips or spoon into
romaine leaves.

Tacos or Burritos

Fantastic Taco Mix
1 can organic fat-free refried beans
organic taco shells or burrito wraps
1 can black olives-drained and rinsed-sliced
4 green onions-chopped
Tofutti Sour Cream
romaine lettuce-sliced thin
tomatoes-chopped

Prepare taco mix per package directions. Fill shells or burrito wraps.

Not Salisbury Steak

BOCA Vegan Burgers
Cook following package directions.
Serve with Mashed Potatoes and Gravy.

Mashed Potatoes

Potatoes – peeled
Boil potatoes, drain, mash with almond or soy milk to desired consistency.

Gravy

¼ c dark miso
2 c water
2 T whole wheat flour
4 T rice milk

Heat miso in water to boiling. Whisk together flour and rice milk. Drizzle flour mix into pan whisking. Lower heat and stir until thickened.

Cooked Vegetables

Cascadian Farms frozen vegetables cooked to package directions.

Mexicalli Rice

By Shirley White
  1 medium tomato
  1/2 c chopped onion
  2 cloves garlic
  2 c cold purified or distilled water
  1 c organic or Basmati rice
  2 T oil
  1 T diced green chili
  1 T chopped cilantro (opt)
  1 tsp. sea salt

Blend tomato, 1/4 cup onion, garlic, and 1 cup water. Rinse the rice once; drain. Heat oil in a frying pan; add rice and 1/4 cup onion. Heat until rice is golden. Add tomato mixture, remaining water and onion, green chili, cilantro, and salt. Cover and simmer for 15 - 20 minutes.

Healthy 4 Him

Veggie Hoagie

by Shirley White
    1/2 c guacamole
    4 sprouted hoagie or sandwich buns, split
    4 slices (3/4 oz. each) organic deli Monterey Jack, soy or rice cheese
    4 slices (3/4-ounce each) organic deli American, soy or rice cheese
    16 thin slices cucumber
    8 thin red bell pepper rings
    8 thin slices tomato
    Coarsely ground pepper

Spread guacamole on cut-sides of buns. Slice cheeses in half diagonally. To assemble each sandwich, layer bottom half of each bun with 2 halves monterey jack cheese, 4 slices cucumber, 2 pepper rings, 2 halves American cheese and 2 slices tomato; sprinkle with pepper. Top each with remaining bun half. Top with Ken's Sweet Vidalia Onion Dressing.

Sloppy Joes

    Fantastic Sloppy Joe Mix
    whole grain buns

Make according to pkg instructions. Serve with cut veggies.

Chili

    Fantastic Chili Mix
    organic chili beans

Make according to pkg instructions. Serve with salad and cornbread.

Burgers

Hamburger Style GardenBurgers or BOCA Burgers
Whole grain or Ezekiel sprouted buns
Nayonaise
Organic ketchup
mustard
romaine lettuce
tomato

Steamed Swiss Chard
1 lb swiss chard-sliced into 1" strips
3 cloves garlic minced (optional)
juice of 1 lemon

Heat 1/2 inch of water in a large skillet. Press in garlic. Add chard. Cover and steam 5 minutes. Turn off heat and add lemon juice.

Steamed Swiss Chard Salad

Steamed Swiss Chard (above)
red bell pepper-diced
tomato-diced
celery-diced
onion-diced

Fold in vegetables after adding lemon juice.

Healthy 4 Him

Mexican Barley Rice

1 c sprouted barley - 1 day until chewable
   (cook it if you're in a hurry)
4 tomatoes-chopped
1/2 an onion -chopped
2 cloves garlic-minced
1/2 tsp sea salt
3 green chilis-chopped
pinch cayenne
¼ c honey
1 jalapeno-chopped
2 T olive oil
1 T parsley

Mix all and marinate 2 hours before eating.

Olive Oil Potato Salad

by Randa John
   potatoes-peeled
   onion-chopped
   curly parsley-chopped
   garlic-crushed or garlic powder
   olive oil and/or flax oil mix
   lemon juice

Boil potatoes, cube and cool. Add rest to taste. Cool and serve.

Luna Salad

2 c lentils-cooked until mushy and drained
10-15 raw macadamia nuts or cashews
juice of 1 lemon
1 small onion-chopped
1 stalk celery-chopped

Blend the macadamia nuts with lemon juice in the food processor until creamy. Stir in with the lentils. Stir in onion and celery. Serve over bed of chopped romaine lettuce and top with cherry tomatoes.

Fettush

2 whole wheat pita breads-toasted then broken into bite-sized pieces
1 cucumber-chopped
4 green onions-chopped
3 tomatoes-chopped
½ bunch parsley
1 clove garlic-crushed
2 T dried mint
juice of 3 lemons
½ c olive oil
raw olives to taste
romaine lettuce

Mix pitas, cucumber, onions, tomatoes and parsley. In separate bowl, make dressing with garlic, mint, lemon juice, and oil. Pour over veggie mix. Serve immediately over bed of romaine lettuce garnished with raw olives. For raw version, leave out pitas and for low-fat, lower the amount of olive oil.

Lentils and Rice with Cucumber Salad
Corbin's (12) Favorite Dinner

  2 c lentils-cooked to package directions
  2 c Jasmine Rice-cooked to package directions
  Sweet onions-grilled in skillet with Earth Balance Buttery Spread

Salad:
  4 tomatoes-chopped large
  2 cucumbers-chopped large
  1 red bell pepper-chopped large
  2 green onions-chopped
  1 T dried mint
  juice of 1 lemon
  4 T olive oil
  dash of garlic powder

Mix salad ingredients and chill one hour. Serve over hot lentils and rice topped with grilled onions.

Tabouli

  Fantastic Tabouli Mix
  curly parsley
  tomatoes-chopped
  juice of 1 lemon
  2 green onions

Make tabouli according to package instructions. Add remaining ingredients and chill 1 hour before eating.

Fruity Tabouli

Fantastic Tabouli Mix
½ c dried apricots-diced
½ c sliced almonds
1 apple-diced
1 T lemon juice
2 green onions
1 T parsley
1 T mint (opt.)
1 T oil-flax, Udo's, hemp, almond or walnut

Make tabouli according to package instructions. Add rest. Chill 1 hour.

Cucumber Sandwich

thick slices of cucumber
thick slices of tomato
sprouts
Ezekiel Bread
Nayonaise or mustard or hummus

Healthy 4 Him

Hummus Sandwiches

Ryan (9) likes Red Pepper Hummus and Corbin (12) Garlic Hummus

> Alvarado Street or Food for Life Sprouted Grain Breads
> Your favorite hummus
> Lettuce leaves
> Slices of tomato
> Slices of onion

Hummus

> 1 can organic chickpeas-drained
> 1 T raw tahini
> juice of 1 lemon
> water if needed to blend

Blend in food processor until thick and creamy.

Garlic Hummus

> 1 can organic chickpeas-drained
> 1 T raw tahini
> juice of 1 lemon
> 2 cloves garlic or more to taste
> water if needed to blend

Blend in food processor until thick and creamy.

Red Pepper Hummus

1 can organic chickpeas-drained
1 T raw tahini
juice of 1 lemon
1 red bell pepper
water if needed to blend

Blend in food processor until thick and creamy.

Pesto Hummus

1 can organic chickpeas-drained
1 T raw tahini
juice of 1 lemon
2 T fresh basil
2 cloves garlic
water if needed to blend

Blend in food processor until thick and creamy.

Spinach Hummus

1 can organic chickpeas-drained
1 T raw tahini
juice of 1 lemon
1 handful fresh spinach
water if needed to blend

Blend in food processor until thick and creamy.

Sun-Dried Tomato Hummus

1 can organic chickpeas-drained
1 T raw tahini
juice of 1 lemon
2 sun-dried tomatoes-rehydrated in water and drained
½ tsp dried Italian Seasoning
water if needed to blend

Blend in food processor til thick and creamy.

Lentil Salad

3 c lentils-cooked
2 carrots-diced
1 red bell pepper-diced
1 stalk celery-diced
1 tomato-diced
1 onion-diced
1 clove garlic-pressed
juice of 2 lemons
2-4 T flax or olive oil
big handful fresh parsley-chopped
1/8 tsp cayenne

Mix all and let it sit for 2 hours or more before eating.

Chickpea Salad

Chickpeas
Olive oil (optional)
Honey, stevia or maple syrup
Lemon juice
Carrots-chopped
Celery-chopped   Mix all to taste.
Onion-chopped
Parsley

Rice

brown rice or brown basmati rice, white jasmine or basmati rice

Boil water per package directions for brown rice but only put in half of what it calls for. Cook 10 minutes then add the other half but as white rice. Continue cooking per package directions.

Cabbage Roll Stew

1- 28 oz can tomatoes	1 head cabbage-chopped
3 T honey	1c cooked brown rice
Juice of 1 Lemon	1 can kidney beans-drained
1 onion-chopped	1 large onion, chopped fine
1/2 tsp celery seeds	½ c parsley
1/2 tsp allspice	1 T sage
1 c water or veg broth	

Mix all in a large pot and cook one hour 'til rice is tender

Potato Cabbage Soup

A kid favorite at our house!

    1 3-lb bag Yukon gold potatoes-hunked
    1 c pearl onions or big chopped onions
    1 head cabbage-sliced thick
    1 T Vegebase broth mix
    4 c water

Boil water with Vegebase and potatoes until fork tender. Add onions and cabbage, cook until cabbage is done-about 20 minutes. Stir to smash a bit of the potatoes to make the soup creamy.
(My kids love this stuff after a big bowl of cut veggies.)

Ethiopian Lentils

1 pound lentils
6 c water or vegetable broth
6 c mild green chiles-chopped
2 red onions-chopped
2 cloves garlic-minced, or more
2 T berebere

Mix all in a large pot and cook one hour 'til lentils are tender.

Berebere

2 tsp. cumin seed
1 tsp. cardamom seed (take out of husks)
1/2 tsp. whole allspice (or ground)
1 tsp. fenugreek seed (or ground)
1 tsp. coriander seed (or ground)
8 whole cloves
1 tsp. black peppercorns
5 tsp. red pepper flakes or crumbled dried red peppers
1 T grated fresh gingeroot (or 1/2 tsp. dried)
1 tsp. túmeric
1 tsp. salt
3 T paprika
1/2 tsp. cinnamon

Toast the seeds and whole cloves in a small frying pan for 2 minutes, stirring constantly-it will be strong and make your eyes burn so open the window and turn on the fans!
Grind the spices in a coffee grinder. Stir in the remaining ingredients. Place in a tightly covered container and freeze. It can be used with lentils or with just about any combination of beans and vegetables.

HEALTHY 4 HIM

Lentil Kale Soup
by Corbin Wandling (12)

    2 c dry lentils
    1 big bunch Kale- chopped
    3 big potatos - chopped
    2 carrots - chopped
    2 cloves garlic - pressed
    4 T salt-free vegetable powder
    1 stalk celery - chopped
    2 small onions - chopped
    1/2 tsp. celery seed
    Dash red pepper flakes
    Water to cover

Put a lid on it and simmer one hour

Garlic Bread
by Corbin Wandling (12)

    Alvarado Street or Ezekiel Sprouted Breads
    Earth Balance Buttery Spread
    Fresh garlic

Press garlic into room temperature spread & mix well. Spread onto bread and toast in the oven.

SWEETS

Healthy 4 Him

Smoothies by Dad

Frozen bananas
Frozen berries
Soy or rice milk
Organic Chocolate syrup

Carob Icing and Graham Crackers

By Ryan Wandling age 9

2 c Cashews-soaked in water 2 hours and drained
½ c carob powder
1/2-1 c maple syrup

Blend all in the food processor and spread onto whole wheat organic graham crackers. If too thin add more cashews; if too thick, add more syrup.

Banana Bread

By Robin Brubaker

    4-6 ripe bananas-smashed
    2 T ground flax seeds soaked in water to cover
    1 tsp vanilla
    ½ c Earth Balance Buttery Spread-melted
    3 T rice milk mixed with 1 T raw apple cider vinegar
    1-1/2 c whole wheat pastry flour
    1 c turbinado sugar
    1 tsp baking soda

Mix bananas, flax, vanilla and spread. Stir in rice milk mix. Mix remaining ingredients together then add to banana mix. Grease pan with Earth Balance, and bake at 350 degrees for one hour.

Banana Black Cherry Chocolate Smoothie

    2 bananas
    2 T organic concentrated black cherry juice
    2 ice cubes
    ½ c almond, rice or soy milk
    organic chocolate syrup or carob powder to taste

Blend and serve.

Healthy 4 Him

Vegan Junk Food
Michael Season's Chips
Barbara's Snackimals
Soy Delicious Ice Cream
Sesame sticks
Quorn Nuggets and Patties
Boca Burgers

Bottled Dressings

I have found a few bottled dressing that I think are "acceptable" for days when life doesn't let you make your own!

DREW'S
Carey Randall's
NASOYA
Seeds of Change
Spectrum
Newman's Own Olive Oil Vinaigrette

RAW RECIPES

Spinach Lasagna
5 c cashews-soaked 2 hours
1 lb baby spinach
juice of 2 lemons
2 c sundried tomatoes
2 T mix of basil and oregano
½ tsp fennel seeds

SMOOTHIE TIPS:

Have fun with it!

If it's not sweet enough, add a drop of liquid stevia or a tablespoon or two of a concentrated fruit juice or date.

Add more ice cubes for colder smoothie.

Use frozen bananas for thicker smoothie.

Hide a few pieces of celery in smoothies.

Hide ground flax seeds in smoothies.

Double or even triple a recipe and make a whole meal out of it.

Carry a smoothie in a thermos to work, on a long bike ride or a hike.

Let the kids make their own; you'll be amazed at how much fruit they will consume!

Cantelope Shake

1-2 cantelopes - peeled and seeded

Blend cantelope flesh.
Great drink for the thermos in summertime!

Apple Ginger Cinnamon Juice

6 apples
1" ginger
cinnamon

Juice apples and ginger. Sprinkle with cinnamon and serve.

Pineapple/Celery Slushy

1 pineapple-peeled and cored
2 stalks celery
1 tray ice cubes

Chop celery then blend with pineapple and ice.
Super refreshing!

Orange Banana Smoothies

Run peeled oranges through the Champion with the blank screen in or use the blender.
Keep in the freezer.
Scoop out some frozen oranges and blend them with a couple frozen bananas.
Add soy, rice or almond milk if you want for a creamier smoothie.

Healthy 4 Him

Banana Tangerine Smoothie

  2 bananas
  2 tangerines-peeled and seeded
  ¼ c shredded coconut
  4 ice cubes
  ½ c water

Blend and serve.

Banana Grape Smoothie

By Ryan Wandling age 9
  2 bananas
  2 T organic concentrated grape juice
  2 ice cubes
  ½ c almond, soy milk or water

Blend and serve.

Banana Black Cherry Smoothie

  2 bananas
  2 T organic concentrated black cherry juice
  2 ice cubes
  ½ c almond, soy milk or water

Blend and serve.

Banana Pineapple Smoothie

2 bananas
½ a pineapple
4 ice cubes
2 T shredded coconut
½ c water

Blend and serve.

Banana Mango Smoothie

2 bananas
1 mango
4 ice cubes
½ c water

Blend and serve.

Banana Strawberry Smoothie

2 bananas
1 c strawberries
2 ice cubes
½ c almond, soy milk or water
½ tsp vanilla

Blend and serve.

Healthy 4 Him

Banana Strawberry Chocolate Smoothie

By Corbin Wandling age 12

    2 bananas
    1 c strawberries
    2 ice cubes
    ½ c almond, soy milk or water
    organic chocolate syrup or carob powder to taste

Blend and serve.

Banana Cherry Smoothie

    2 bananas
    1 c cherries-pitted
    2 ice cubes
    ½ c almond, soy milk or water
    ½ tsp vanilla

Blend and serve.

Grape Slushy

By Dave and Val Rodenbucher

    1 bunch grapes-red or green
    1 stalk celery

Blend and serve.
(I like to half-freeze it before eating.)

Everyday Juice

5 lbs carrots
1 beet with greens
1 stalk celery
2 leaves greens-kale, collards, spinach or turnip
2 apples

Juice all and serve. Freeze leftovers.

Carrot Beet Juice

By Denise Meyer

10 carrots
1/2 large red beet
beet greens
handful parsley
handful spinach
1/2 cucumber
3 stalks of celery.

Juice and serve. It's yummy!

Almond Milk

> 2c raw almonds
> Water to cover

Soak almonds overnight in water. Drain.

> 2-4 dates
> More water to cover
> Vanilla bean-goo from center

Blend all 'til milky consistency. Strain with cheesecloth or fine mesh strainer.

MEALS

Healthy 4 Him

Spinach Lasagna

5 c cashews-soaked 2 hours
1lb baby spinach
juice of 2 lemons
2 c sundried tomatoes
2 T mix of basil and oregano
½ tsp fennel seeds
1-2 cloves garlic
water to blend

Blend in food processor – cashews and lemon juice until creamy/cheesy. Stir in spinach. Pour into casserole dish.
Blend tomatoes and herbs with water until thick sauce.
Spread over casserole. Serve with a nice big green salad.
Beware-this is really good but high in fat!

Bill's Big Mushroom Pizza

by Bill MacGee

Several big portabella mushroom caps
Your favorite guacamole
Sprouts
Red bell peppers - sliced

Top mushroom caps with guacamole, sprouts and peppers. Cut each in forths.

Collard Burritos

By Peter Fulda

> Large fresh collard green leaves
> Add for every leaf of collard green,
> 1 tsp miso
> 1/8 - ¼ medium ripe tomato
> ½ inch length of cucumber
> 1/3 green onion
> 3 T raw sunflower and/or sesame seeds
> 3 T sprouts of any kind
> 1 T ground flax seeds
> 1 T leek or radish

Spread a bead of miso along the center vein of each collard green leaf. Mince other vegetables and grind flax seeds. Add, together with seeds into collard leaf over bead of miso, fold up into burrito wrap and enjoy! Contents of burrito may be substituted with other items you can find in your refrigerator.

Kohl-Slaw

> kohlrabi-shredded
> Tahini Dressing (pg. 94)

Mix and serve over romaine.
Can top with slivered red bell pepper or raw olives or sunflower seeds... whatever you want.

Healthy 4 Him

Nappa Salad

    1 head nappa cabbage-sliced thin
    1 onion, sliced thin
Dressing:
    ½ c shoyu or tamari
    1/8-1/4 tsp cayenne
    1/8 c raw honey or 1 date blended with water
    ½ " ginger-minced
    1 clove garlic-pressed
    juice of 1 orange

Mix dressing with a fork and toss with salad.

Susie Q's Slaw

By Sue Porter
    3/4 small cabbage-shredded
    2 small beets-grated
    2 small carrots-grated
    1 stalk celery-chopped fine
    4 green onions-chopped fine
    2 T sunflower seeds
    juice of 1 lemon
    ½ c raw honey or 4-6 dates blended with water
    ½ c raw apple cider vinegar or lemon juice
    shoyu to taste

Mix all and enjoy!

Oops, I'm Outta Lettuce Salad

Salad:

All the veggies from the bottom of your fridge-chopped small in the food processor. (Today I used broccoli, red bell pepper, kohlrabi, onion, celery, carrot.) Add a handful of sunflower and/or pumpkin seeds.

Dressing:

> 4 T whatever kind of nut butter you have
>
> juice of 1 lime or 1 lemon or 2 T raw apple cider vinegar
>
> garlic powder to taste
>
> pinch of cayenne or splash of hot sauce

Whisk dressing with a fork and toss with salad!

Colorful Cauliflower Salad

By Linda DePue, HM

> 1 head cauliflower, cut into pieces

A combination of any or all of the following:

> bell peppers, diced:
>
> 1 red pepper
>
> 1 orange pepper
>
> 1 yellow pepper
>
> 1 green pepper
>
> 1 small sweet onion, chopped
>
> 1 c Veganaise or Nayonaise
>
> 1/3 c apple cider vinegar
>
> 2-4 T honey

Mix and chill.

My Old August Salad-RAW

6 tomatoes-thin sliced
1 big sweet onion-thin sliced
1 red bell pepper-thin sliced
1 zucchini-thin sliced
fresh basil leaves (optional)

Dressing:
1 tomato
1 clove garlic
juice of 1 lemon
dash of cayenne

Blend dressing in food processor or blender and pour over salad. Let it sit for an hour or so to blend flavors.

Nappa Almond Slaw

Dressing:
¼ c raw almond butter
1 clove garlic
juice of 2 limes
water to thin

Salad:
¼ c fresh cilantro
¼ c fresh mint
4 green onions-minced
1 carrot-shaved
1 head nappa cabbage-shredded
1 red bell pepper-thin sliced

Whisk dressing and toss with salad.

Celery Root Salad

1 celery root-peeled and shredded
2 apples-shredded
1 c walnuts-chopped
½ c raisins
1 c Veganaise or NutDressing
¼ c honey

Mix all and serve.

Mom's Cranberry Salad

By Gloria Eden
1-2 bags cranberries- chopped in food processor
3 stalks celery-chopped fine
pecans
apples-chopped fine
raisins
Sauce:
2 bananas
2 ripe pears
4 dates

Blend the sauce in the food processor and stir into the salad. Add raw honey if it is still too sour.

Linda's Favorite Salad

By Linda Vaughan
  4-6 cups baby greens
  1/2c fresh parsley-chopped
  1 leaf of kale-chopped (optional)
  1 avocado-diced
  ¼ red onion-sliced thin
  ¼ green pepper-sliced thin (optional)
  6T walnuts-chopped
  a good handful of raisins

Tossed with Udo's Oil, raw apple cider vinegar.

Party Size Enchilada Salad

  2 jalapenos-diced
  1/2 an onion-diced
  2 cloves garlic-pressed
  1 date blended with water
  2 T cumin seeds-ground or ground cumin
  2 T dried oregano
  8 avocadoes-diced
  4 tomatoes-diced
  1 c fresh cilantro
  ¼ c fresh lime juice
  Romaine Lettuce

Mix all except lettuce and marinate for 1 hour. Serve over lettuce or roll up into large lettuce leaves.

Minty Peas

1 lb sugar snap peas-chopped
3 T onion-diced
juice of 1/2 a lemon
1 tsp raw honey
1 tsp dijon mustard
1- ½ c fresh mint leaves-chopped

Mix all and marinate 1 hour before serving.

Herbed Radishes

16 radishes-sliced thick
1 cucumber-sliced
16 cherry tomatoes-sliced in half
juice of 1/2 a lemon
4 T olive oil (optional)
¾ c fresh basil
2 T fresh dill

Mix all and marinade 1 hour.

Healthy 4 Him

Minty Carrots

    1 lb carrots-grated
    ¼ c raisins
    2/3 c fresh mint
    juice of 1/2 a lemon
    ¼ c olive oil (optional)

Mix all and marinate 1 hour.

Horsey Cabbage and Beets

    4 c cabbage-chopped
    4 beets-shredded
    1 c fresh grape juice
    1 T lemon juice
    1 c horseradish-grated
    1 c raw apple cider vinegar
    1 T pepper
    1 tsp salt
    ¼ tsp cayenne

Mix all and marinate 1 hour.

Backyard Pesto Salad

Dressing:
- ½ c fresh basil
- ½ c fresh oregano
- ¼ c fresh mint
- 2 cloves garlic
- juice of 1 lemon
- 1/4 of a red onion-chopped
- ¼ c pine nuts
- water to thin

Salad:
- Backyard greens-dandelion, baby greens, lettuces-whatever you planted.
- olives
- cherry tomatoes

Tomato Chutney

- 5 tomatoes-chopped
- 3 onions-chopped
- 1 green pepper-chopped
- 1 hot or sweet red pepper-chopped
- 4 tart apples-chopped
- ¾ c raisins
- 1/3 c raw honey (optional)
- ½ c raw apple cider vinegar or lemon juice
- 1 tsp or more curry powder

Mix all and marinate 1 hour.

Snow Peas with Cashews

1 T shoyu
1/2 tsp red pepper flakes
1 tsp maple syrup
1 T olive oil
1 lb snow peas-chopped
¼ c raw cashews
3 cloves garlic
1 T gingerroot-grated
2 green onions-chopped
1 T lemon juice

Mix all and marinate 2 hours or overnight.

Basiled Sugar Snap Peas

1 lb sugar snap peas-stringed
2 T olive oil
2 T fine chopped walnuts
2 T fresh shredded basil

Mix all and marinate 2 hours.

Greek Peppers

2 T olive oil
4 bell peppers-red, yellow and/or orange-cut into chunks
2 cloves garlic-crushed
2 T lemon juice
8 large kalamata olives-whole
1 tsp fresh oregano

Mix all and marinate 2 hours. Pour over a big bed of romaine and serve.

Orange Salad

2 oranges-seeded, chopped
1 tsp honey
8 radishes-thin circles
1/2 tsp paprika

Mix all and marinate 1 hour.

Daikon Radishes

1-1/2 lbs daikon radishes-shredded
2 T shoyu
1 T lemon juice
1 date blended with water
1 tsp sesame oil
1 T sesame seeds

Mix and serve immediately. (Note: This does not keep; it waters out.)

Maple Turnips and Carrots

  1 lb turnips-peeled and cubed
  3 carrots-circles
  2 T maple syrup or 1 date blended with water

Mix all and marinate 2 hours.

Spiced Turnips

  2 T olive oil
  1 onion-ringed
  1-1/2 lbs turnips-peeled and cubed
  2 tomatoes-diced
  ½ tsp cumin
  2 T cilantro or parsley
  juice of 1 lime

Mix all and marinate 2 hours.

Curried Turnip Slaw

  1 large turnip-shredded
  ½ a small head of cabbage-shredded
  1 small red onion-shredded
  2T pumpkin seeds
  1T Udo's Oil
  juice of 2 limes
  1 tsp curry powder
  2T maple syrup or 1 date blended with water

Mix all and marinate 2 hours.

Cabbage with Lemon/Dill Cashew Butter

    several large cabbage leaves
    sprouts
Cashew Cream:
    1c raw cashews-soak in water overnight in the fridge
    1 tsp dried dill
    1/8 tsp garlic powder
    1/8 tsp onion powder or dried onion
    juice of 1 lemon

Drain cashews then blend with remaining ingredients til creamy.
Spread cream onto cabbage leaves, fill with sprouts or your favorite chopped veggies, roll and eat.

Oranges and Avocados

    2 oranges-peeled, sectioned and sliced in half
    1 avocados-peeled and cubed
    4 radishes-diced
    1 T lime juice
    1tsp chili powder

Mix all and marinade 1 hour.

Healthy 4 Him

Pam's Beet Salad

by Pam Fretz

> **4** beets-shredded
> **4** carrots-shredded
> **1** c pineapple-diced
> **½** c raisins

Mix all and let sit 2 hours for flavors to blend.

Minted Nappa Cabbage

> **1** head nappa cabbage-cut into thin strips
> **2** carrots-shredded
> **12** fresh basil leaves-shredded
> **12** fresh mint leaves-shredded
> **2** T cilantro
> **2** T lime juice
> **1-1/2** T shoyu (optional)
> **1** tsp red pepper flakes or cayenne
> **1** T maple syrup
> **¼** c cashews

Mix all and marinate 1 hour.

Spiced Cucumbers

3 cucumbers-circles
½ c raw apple cider vinegar or lemon juice
¼ c olive oil (optional)
3 T maple syrup
1 tsp red pepper flakes or 1 fresh red chili pepper
2 T minced red onion
2 T cashews (optional)

Mix all and marinate 1 hour.

Lemony Cukes

3 cucumbers-circles
2 T olive oil (optional)
3 shallots-minced
2 T lemon juice
2 T fresh mint leaves-shredded

Mix all and marinate 1 hour.

Cucumbers and Watermelon

2 T lemon juice
2 tsp maple syrup
1 tsp red pepper flakes
2 cucumbers-circles
2 c watermelon-seeded and diced
¼ c red onion-minced
2 T mint leaves-shredded

Mix all and chill 1 hour.

Marinated Dandelion Greens

10 c dandelion greens-stemmed and chopped
Marinade:
3 T olive oil
2 shallots-minced
2 T raw apple cider vinegar

Heat marinade and pour over greens. Let wilt and serve. Top with chopped nuts-optional.

Chili Lime Onions

10 green pablano or mild chilis-cut into thin strips
4 big white onions-ringed
4 limes-juiced
1/2 tsp oregano
2 T maple syrup

Mix all and marinate 2 hours. Great served simply over a bed of romaine lettuce.

Taco Crackers or Taco Balls

1-1/2 c taco sauce (pg. 100)
2 c ground filberts or walnuts
1/8 c ground flax seeds

Mix all, press onto teflex dehydrator sheets, score with pizza cutter turned cracker scorer, dry until flippable, flip and finish drying until crispy crackers. Or, drop by the 1/2 tsp and dehydrate until like meatballs.

Taco Salad

romaine lettuce-cut thin
green onions
black olives-drained and rinsed-sliced
tomatoes-chopped
Taco Balls (pg. 79)
Taco Sauce (pg. 100)
guacamole

Butternut Squash Soup

1 butternut squash-peeled, seeded and cubed
1 c pine nuts-soaked in water 1 hour and drained
2 tsp cinnamon
1/2 tsp nutmeg
1/2 tsp allspice
1/2 tsp ginger
¼ c maple syrup or more to taste
1 avocado

Blend all, adding water to thin to desired consistency. Can be heated on very low heat til warm.

Walnut Stuffing

2 c walnuts
1 c pecans
½ c almonds
1 onion
2 stalks celery
1 T sage
1/2 tsp rosemary
1/2 tsp thyme
1 clove garlic

Blend all in food processor until it sticks together like stuffing. Taste and add more seasonings if needed.

Gravy

¼ c garbanzo miso
1/2 small onion
2 cloves garlic
1/2 a jalapeno
4 dates
1 T shoyu
juice of 1 orange
juice of 1 lemon
water to thin

Blend all in food processor adding water to thin.

Mashed Cauliflower

1 head cauliflower
1 c pine nuts or cashews
juice of 4 lemons
1/2 tsp thyme
¼ c walnut oil (optional)
water

Blend all in food processor adding water to thin til fluffy.

Fruity Wild Rice

2 c sprouted wild rice-3 days until chewable (cook it if you're in a hurry)
¼ c dried cranberries
¼ c raisins
¼ c celery-chopped
¼ c onion-chopped
¼ c olive oil (optional)
2 T maple syrup
slivered almonds and parsley to garnish

Acorn Apple Soup

1 acorn squash-peeled and cubed
2 T olive oil
2 leek whites
1 rib celery
1 apple
1-1/2 c water
½ c raw apple cider vinegar
1 tsp fresh ginger root
1/2 tsp ground ginger
1/2 tsp curry powder
1/2 tsp cumin
1/4 tsp cardamom
1/4 tsp nutmeg
chopped walnuts for garnish

Blend all in food processor or blender until creamy.

SNACKS

Healthy 4 Him

The Gold Mine

By Caitlyn Storrow, age 10
> core the middle out of an apple
> spread almond butter inside the apple
> plug the ends with raisins or dates(optional)
> put an almond on each end
> Bon appetit!

Cut Veggies

by Ryan Wandling, age 8
> broccoli
> black olives
> cauliflower
> baby carrots
> cherry, grape or sugar drop tomatoes
> Your favorite dressing for dip.

Celery and Dates

By Dave Rodenbucher
> celery
> medjool dates

Cut celery into 3 inch strips.
Cut dates into 3 inch strips.
Lay dates strips into celery strips!
My favorite munchy!

Kohlrabi

I love kohlrabi!
kohlrabi

Cut off leaves, save for juices.
Peel kohlrabi with a sharp knife.
Slice to eat or eat like an apple!
Tastes like celery/potato/turnip mix.

Jalapeno Cashews

raw cashews
jalapeno hot sauce (pg. 94)

Soak cashews in hot sauce for 1 hour then dehydrate until crispy.

Pickles-Garlic/Kosher

By Carol Giambri, HM
any kind of pickles sliced thin and/or peeled
olive oil
apple cider vinegar
garlic
dill-fresh/dried
pickle seasonings
bay leaf

Place all in bowl or jar....let sit....or eat right away. Enjoy.
Variations: can add Italian seasonings, fresh onions or whatever you think a pickle should taste like.

Raw Olives

olives in brine

You will find these in Lebanese or Italian markets. Soak them in pure water for a day or two rinsing and refilling often. This takes much of the salt out. When you get them where you want them-don't bother tasting until the next day or you might swell up like I did the first time I made them. Dress them with a teaspoon of olive oil, a pinch of cayenne and orange zest. You can also dress them with olive oil, thyme and lemon zest. I like to add like 5 of these to my salad and forego the dressing altogether sometimes.

Buckwheat Pizza Crackers

Adapted from The Raw Food Guy

4 c hulled buckwheat groats, soaked 2 hours in water just to cover-don't drain

1 c sun-dried tomatoes, soaked in water

2 T pizza seasoning or combo of basil, oregano, parsley

2 cloves garlic

1 small onion

2 T olive oil

Blend all in food processor until thick and creamy. Stir to mix well.
Scoop out by heaping teaspoonfuls onto teflex dehydrator sheets or parchment paper. Tap the tray on the counter to flatten crackers a bit. Dry for 6-8 hours, flip and dry another 4-6 hours until crispy.

Buckwheat Mini Pizzas

Buckwheat Pizza Crackers
pizza sauce
olives-sliced
onions-chopped

Spread sauce on crackers and top with olives and onions or whatever you like. Or just dip the crackers in the sauce!

Stuffed Mushrooms

25 mushrooms-brushed clean, stems removed
mushroom stems
1/2c pine nuts
1/2c walnuts
2T Italian Seasoning
1 clove garlic
1T minced onion
1 tomato

Blend all except mushrooms in the food processor til thick and smooth.
Spoon into mushroom caps.
Dehydrate at 105 degrees for 3-4 hours.

Healthy 4 Him

Trail Mix

    raw almonds
    raw sunflower seeds
    raw pumpkin seeds
    raw walnuts
    banana chips
    dates
    figs
    dried apricots
    raisins

Corbin's Trail Mix

    pecans
    banana chips
    sesame sticks
    raisins
    raw macadamia nuts

Cinnamon Nuts

    raw almonds or pecans
    oil-flax, Udo's, hemp, almond or walnut
    raw honey
    cinnamon
    a few drops of stevia (optional)

Mix nuts to coat and taste. Dehydrate until crispy.

Howard's Banana Coconut Cookies

by The RawFood Guy

bananas
unsweetened, unsulphured shredded coconut
walnuts-chopped
raisins

Blend a bunch of bananas in the food processor, add coconut until it holds together, stir in walnuts and raisins. Put out onto a teflex dehydrator sheet. Cover with parchment paper and roll out with a rolling pin. Score with a pizza cutter turned cookie scorer and dry until crispy. No need to flip. Break into squares and enjoy!

Oriental Snack Mix

raw cashews
raw sunflower seeds
raw pumpkin seeds
Just Peas
raw unhulled sesame seeds
dried onion
garlic cloves-press in
oil-flax, Udo's, hemp, sesame, almond or walnut
flax seeds-ground
cayenne powder
nama shoyu or tamari
a few drops of stevia (optional)
hulled buckwheat groats (optional)

Mix all together to your taste and to coat. Dehydrate until crispy.

Healthy 4 Him

Mexican Snack Mix

   raw almonds-rough chopped
   raw walnuts-rough chopped
   Just Corn
   oil-flax, Udo's, hemp, almond or walnut-drizzled
   garlic cloves-pressed in or dried garlic
   hot sauce
   cayenne powder
   a few drops of stevia (optional)
   hulled buckwheat groats (optional)

Mix all together to your taste and to coat. Dehydrate until crispy.

Dilly Snack Mix

   sliced almonds
   hulled buckwheat groats (optional)
   dried celery
   Just Mixed Veggies
   dried onions
   garlic cloves-pressed in or dried garlic
   oil-flax, Udo's, hemp, almond or walnut-drizzled
   dried dill
   dried parsley
   a few drops of stevia (optional)

Candied Macadamias

raw Macadamia nuts
maple syrup

Soak the nuts in syrup to coat for 2 hours. Lay out onto mesh dehydrator sheets. Dry overnight.

Lemony Brazil Nuts

raw brazil nuts
lemon juice
dried thyme
lemon pepper

Squeeze juice over brazil nuts to coat. Add seasonings and soak for 2 hours. Lay out onto mesh dehydrator sheets. Dry overnight.

Wicked Walnuts

walnuts
hot sauce of choice

Soak walnuts in hot sauce for 2 hours. Dehydrate overnight until crunchy. Tastes like cheese puffs!

DRESSINGS & SAUCES

Healthy 4 Him

Tahini Dressing

    2 T tahini
    juice of 1 lemon
    1 clove garlic
    water to blend

Blend in food processor or blender.

Tahini Jalapeno Dressing

    2 T tahini
    juice 1 lemon
    1 clove garlic
    ¼ tsp fresh jalapeno or Jalapeno Hot Sauce

Blend in food processor or blender.

Jalapeno Hot Sauce

    jalapenos-cut off stems only
    apple cider vinegar
    kosher salt

Put jalapenos in a large pot. Cover halfway with vinegar and add a T of salt for every 2 c vinegar. Cook until peppers are soft-a good 2 hours. Let cool. Place all in a blender and liquefy.

Jalapeno Honey Mustard Dressing

2 T Dijon mustard
2 T honey
½ tsp Jalapeno Hot Sauce
3 leaves fresh sage chopped (optional)

Interesting Guacamole

3 ripe avocados
1 small onion, minced
2 small tomatoes, chopped
juice of 1 lemon
1/4 tsp salt or to taste
1/2 clove garlic, minced
1/2 tsp pepper or to taste
1/2 tsp ground cinnamon
1/4 - 1/2 tsp chili powder
1/4 - 1/2 tsp ground cumin

Blend in food processor.

Healthy 4 Him

Deb's Guac!

By Debra Garrison
>2 ripe avocados
>1 medium-large ripe tomato
>1/4-1/2 of a medium-large onion
>sprinkle of cayenne
>triple-quadruple sprinkle of fresh ground black pepper
>double-triple sprinkle of dried cilantro
>1/8-1/4 tsp garlic powder

Mix everything together and enjoy!

Tomato Vinaigrette

>tomatoes-chopped
>fresh oregano-chopped
>fresh basil-chopped
>lemon juice
>olive oil

Squeeze lemons, add salt and whisk in olive oil. Add fresh chopped tomatoes, oregano and basil. Great served over chopped zucchini or romaine.

Nut Dressing Base

>1 c any nuts-soaked 4 hours and drained
>juice of 1 lemon
>options: add pinch cayenne, parsley, dried onion, garlic, dill,

Blend in food processor until creamy.

Pizza Sauce

2 c sun-dried tomatoes-soaked in water 2 hours or until soft enough
to blend-save water to blend
2 T pizza seasoning or combo of basil, oregano and parsley
2 cloves garlic
½ an onion or 1 small onion

Blend all in food processor until thick and creamy.
Serve on slices of zucchini topped with chopped olives and onions.

Cucumber Relish

5 cucumbers-chopped
1/2 a green pepper-chopped
1 onion-chopped
1 apple-chopped
1/2 c raw apple cider vinegar or lemon juice
1 tsp mustard seed
1/2 tsp celery seed
pinch cayenne

Mix all and marinate 1 hour.

Creamy Peach Dressing

1 T parsley
2 peaches-pureed
1/2 a red bell pepper-fine diced
1/2 a yellow bell pepper-fine diced
1/2 an onion-diced fine
juice of 1 lemon
water to thin if necessary.

Mix all and shake to blend.

Celery Salsa

3 ribs celery, chopped
½ c onion, chopped
1/2 c finely sliced green onion
1 jalapeno pepper, finely diced
zest and juice of 1 lime
1 tsp raw honey
1 banana, sliced and diced

Mix all and marinate 1 hour

Red Pepper Spread

2 red bell peppers
½ c walnuts
1 T blackstrap molasses
1 tsp lemon juice
1/4tsp cumin
water to thin

Blend all in food processor until spreadable. Spread on cut veggies.

Spicy Tomato Chutney

3 lbs tomatoes-chopped
1-½ c lemon juice
1-½ c honey or 10 dates blended with water
½ c raisins
1 T cinnamon
1 tsp red pepper flakes or cayenne
1 tsp cloves
1 tsp coriander
1 T ginger root minced

Mix all and marinate 2 hours or overnight.

HEALTHY 4 HIM

Sweet Potato Salsa

1 large sweet potato-peeled and shredded
juice of 1 orange
shot maple syrup
1 tsp shoyu
4 scallions-minced
juice of 1 lime   Mix all and marinate 1 hour.
2 T cilantro

Mexican Onion Relish

2 green chili peppers-seeded and chopped
1 tsp allspice
½ tsp fresh pepper
1 tsp oregano
2 large white onions-chopped
2 cloves garlic-minced
1/3 c lemon juice
½ c raw apple cider vinegar   Mix all and marinate 1 hour.

Taco Sauce

15 sundried tomatoes-soaked in 2 c water 1 hour-save water to blend
6 dates
1 tsp cumin
1 small onion
2 cloves garlic
pinch cayenne

Blend in food processor adding water to thin. Serve on salad burritos, as a salad dressing, whatever!

SWEETS

Applesauce

apples-peeled and cored
cinnamon (opt.)

Run apples through Champion juicer with the blank screen in place or blend in food processor. Stir in cinnamon.

Becky's Ginger Treats

By Becky Lesko
1 lb raisins
1 tsp vanilla
1 tsp ground ginger (or more to taste)
½ tsp allspice
1 c raw almonds-ground fine

Blend raisins, vanilla, ginger and allspice until smooth. Roll into balls and roll in almonds.

Apple Treat

10 apples-peeled
½ tsp cinnamon
scraping from inside a vanilla
1 c raisins

Half blend the apples and add the rest.

Apple Pie

Applesauce (page 102) made with 12 apples-unpeeled or peeled
2 T psyllium hulls
2 c dates-soaked ½ hour in water then drained

Blend in the dates as you make the applesauce. Stir in psyllium.

Crust:
1/2 c almonds
1 c dates
1/2 c walnuts

Chop together in food processor until it holds together loosely but sticky. Press into pie plate, fill and chill for 1 hour until set.

Corbin's Banana Mango Parfait

Crumbles:
3 c almonds-ground in food processor
1 c dates-ground with almonds
Pudding:
5 bananas
5 dates
4 mangos
juice and zest of 3 lemons

Blend pudding ingredients until pudding-like. Layer in a clear glass bowl. Top with sliced strawberries, sliced kiwis and/or blueberries. Can also sprinkle with coconut.

HEALTHY 4 HIM

Seame Bars

3 T honey-heated til runny
1 c sesame seeds
1 c sunflower seeds
½ c raisins
½ c chopped nuts
optional chopped dried fruits

Mix until thick and all coated. Add more honey if necessary but keep thick. Press into cookie sheets and sit out overnight. Cut into bars and enjoy-will be a bit sticky but should hold together nicely. (Just don't let the kids have them in the evening!)

Frozen Black Cherry Banana Pie

12 frozen, peeled bananas
2 c fresh pitted cherries
2-3 T Black Cherry Concentrate (optional)

Run through the Champion Juicer with the blank screen in. Stir in concentrate.

Crust:
½ c raw almonds
4-5 pitted dates (6-7 if small)

Blend until gooey enough to press into a 10" pie plate or springform pan (the Pampered Chef ones work great).
Press crust into pan then fill with banana ice cream. Refreeze just about solid (maybe 4 hours). Garnish with sliced fresh pitted cherries. You can also stir some in for a cherry cordial effect.

SEASONAL SWEETS

January Sweets

Fresh Orange Juice

Buy a case of oranges and squeeze away! Make enough each time to fill a pitcher to store in the fridge. I don't like to use my regular juicer for this - makes it too creamy. Citrus juicers work great but I don't have one yet. I use an old reamer which also leaves a lot of pulp in. Orange juice is a great meal after exercise.

Grapefruit

Mom loves grapefruit. She just slices it down the middle, scores it and eats it with a spoon over a bowl

Pears

Grandma likes them especially for their high fiber content.

Bananas

Great all year long! A nice change in winter to balance out all the citrus.

February Sweets

Mineolas

Peel and eat 'til you are not hungry any more.

Blood Oranges

Peel and eat "til you are not nungry any more.

Healthy 4 Him

Clementines
Ryan's (9) favorite because they are easy to peel. He has been known to eat an entire box by himself!

March Sweets

Strawberries
California strawberries roll in to town this month. Not as good as local and fresh, but a welcome ingredient in Spring!

Pineapple
Oh, man, talk about a meal! I only buy yellow pineapples that smell like pineapple from the bottom end. Cut off the top, cut off the bottom then slice down the outsides to peel then cut around core.

April Sweets

Raspberries
Raspberries make a great snack in April and May!

Bananas
Smoothies, frozen pies . . .

Durian
I hate this stuff but my pal Dave made me put it in because he and his wife Val love it! They cut it open and spoon out the custard (goo).

May Sweets

Papaya

Like papaya or papaya juice? Now is the time to buy them. Try drying the seeds to use ground as seasoning.

Mangos

Keep your eye out for early mangos. Three or four of the smaller ones that are available this time of year make a nice meal.

June Sweets

Strawberries

Find yourself a berry farm that doesn't spray too much and you are good to go picking. On the days we pick, that is all we eat! I like to freeze some then go picking again and again 'til the fields are spent.

Cantaloupe

Cantaloupe is usually the first ripe melon we see in early summer. Cut one in half, scoop out the seeds and enjoy with a spoon right out of its skin bowl.

Healthy 4 Him

July Sweets

Blueberries

You know its blueberry season when they arrive in the stores in boxes rather than half-pints! Our boxes make it home half empty! Don't forget to freeze some for later.

Cherries

What better meal is there than a big bowl of dark cherries? My boys start begging for cherries the first time thay are on the shelf but it is best to wait a few weeks to get the really good ripe sweet ones. The coolest thing is we can afford to buy pounds of cherries when they are in season because we don't buy meat which is expensive all year round.

Blackberries

Here in Ohio we get fresh ripe blackberries from Amish country and they are sooooo yummy.

Sweet Corn

Buy it fresh and young from your local grower then eat it raw!

August Sweets

Mangos

We discovered Kent, Haden, Susie Q and Ataulfo mangos this year. Tommy Atkins are the fibrous, stringy ones most people don't like. Cut them in half down either side of the flat seed. Peel around the seed and eat off excess. Then you can either just dig in eating the flesh out of the skin halves or score the flesh and pop it out. Whatever you do, have a towel handy or eat them over the sink!!!

Grapes

Red, black, globe, green. Mix them in a huge bowl for a beautiful presentation. I have been known to have bags of grapes in my purse!

Plums

We bought so many plums this year. My boys love them - all different kinds.

Peaches and Nectarines

Mmmm, so sweet.

Apricots

Ryan loves apricots. Cute and fuzzy just like him.

September Sweets

Watermelon

Cut one in half or fourths and give each family member a hunk, a towel and a fork!
Dinner is served. We bought them from and old guy on the side of the road several
times this month and they were excellent - only $2.00 each!

Apples

Golden delicious, MacIntosh and Jonathons are usually ripe this month.

Raspberries

Again raspberries are ripening. Fall raspberries are less seedy and more flavorful.

Fresh Figs

To peel or not to peel? Some do some don't. I cut them in half and scoop out the
flesh.

Dates

We like medjool, honey and deglet dates.

Healthy 4 Him

October Sweets

Apples, apples, apples!!!
My new favorite for eating whole is the Melrose.

Musk & Honeydew Melons
My pal Dave syas this is the month to make friends with the local melon farmers. They often have wagon loads selling for $1-2.00 each!

Asian Pears
Asian pears are really neat. They work great in oriental type slalads and are also delicious alone. I peel and core them then slice like an apple. They are hard and crunchy.

Kiwi
Cut in half and eat with a spoon. Ryan loves kiwis.

November Sweets

Hachiya Persimmons
Oh my gosh are these things fabulous! I like the bright orange ones. Wait 'til they are so squishy you can barely pick them up. Then cut one open and suck out the gooey sweet flesh. For a nice meal, simply peel a mess of them (it will make a mess) and put them in a big bowl. They will smoosh together like pudding.

Grapes
Thankfully, grapes are still good November and December.

December Sweets

Cranberries
Juiced cranberries make a nice addition to fresh apple juice.

Star Fruit
Star fruit is a hit in fruit salads.

Pomegranates
Kindly a pain to get to the seeds but worth the effort. A beautiful topping for that fruit salad!

Honey Tangerines
These have a thin peel and should feel full of juice. We cut them in half and scoop out the flesh with our teeth right over the sink! One time, Ryan (age 7 at the time), ate a whole dozen of them for lunch.

Bananas
Always the mainstay!

DAILY MENU POSSIBILITIES

Example 1
water
BarleyMax
carrot/apple/swiss chard
/celery juice
one pineapple
6 oranges
Lemony Brazil Nuts
Taco Salad
Grapes

Example 2
water
BarleyMax
carrot/apple/kale juice
Banana Smoothie
celery and dates
August Salad
plums

Healthy 4 Him

I just put these in order of when I would typically have them in a day when I get hungry. One of the weirdest things for me to get used to was eating when I was hungry and *not* by the clock! There are some basic guidelines to follow here:

1. Drink your Barley, wait awhile then have your juice or mix the two together.

2. Try to get in a good workout in the morning.

3. When you first are hungry for a meal, go for fruit and eat until you are full.

4. If you have sugar issues, eat the fruit with something green like celery or leaf lettuce.

5. Carry some nuts or trail mixes with you so you don't get caught hungry without food!

6. Always carry water.

7. Try one of the recipes in this book for dinner or just have a big green salad.

A big key for me has been to have food ready, salads already prepared in the fridge. I like to take Saturdays and make 3-4 different pre-made salads to have for the next couple of days. Then do it again mid week. Below are some typical days for me. Notice that none of them are even following the same pattern. Sometimes I'll have a big salad for lunch then have bananas for dinner. Again, no big deal. At times I'll add a piece of organic whole grain bread or sprouted bread to my salad meal.

Listed below are some typical (or not-so-typical) days for me:

Example 1

water
BarleyMax
carrot/apple/swiss chard/celery juice
one pineapple
6 oranges
Lemony Brazil Nuts
Taco Salad
Grapes

Example 2

water
BarleyMax
carrot/apple/kale juice
Banana Smoothie
celery and dates
August Salad
plums

Example 3

water
BarleyMax
carrot/apple/collard/beet juice

Healthy 4 Him

8 kiwis
Leftover August Salad (great the next day!) with Marinated
Dandelion Greens
Banana Raspberry Smoothie

Example 4

water
BarleyMax
one cantelope blended like a shake (really filling)
celery with almond butter
Spiced Cucumbers over romaine lettuce with Chili Lime Onions
Raspberries

Example 5

water
fresh squeezed orange juice
4 Mangos
Manna Bread
Mixed Baby Greens with Jalapeno Tahini Dressing
Oriental Snack Mix

Favorite Resources:

www.thecampaign.org
The Campaign to Label Genetically Engineered Foods-Please join!

www.hacres.com
www.madcowboy.com
www.doctorgraham.cc
www.vegsource.com
www.healthy4him.com
www.healthfullivingintl.com
www.drfuhrman.com
www.freedomyou.com
www.livingnutrition.com

http://groups.yahoo.com/groups/hd_diet_club

Healthy 4 Him

INDEX

Healthy 4 Him

Healthy 4 Him

Healthy 4 Him